090262   Art   746.92092
2 week loan

KAMITSIS, LYDIA

Paco Rabanne

1
London: Thames & Hudson,   0500019657

paco rabanne

paco rabanne

Lydia Kamitsis

 Thames & Hudson

Translated from the French by Harriet Mason

This edition first published in the United Kingdom in 1999 by
Thames & Hudson Ltd, 181A High Holborn, London WC1V 7QX

© 1999 Thames & Hudson Ltd, London
Original edition © 1999 Éditions Assouline, Paris

British Library Cataloguing-in-Publication Data
A catalogue record for this book is available from the British Library

ISBN 0-500-01965-7

Printed and bound in Italy

t he 'Jules Verne of couture' and the 'metal worker' are two of the most common nicknames given to Paco Rabanne, the fashion designer who for a time was not even acknowledged as a couturier. Paco Rabanne has worked for more than thirty years in the strictly controlled world of fashion and has an unassailable reputation, but he still falls outside the accepted definition of haute couture, or even that of couture in the wider sense.

His choice of totally different materials to those traditionally used for clothing, his challenge to the 'cut and sewn' formula and his aversion to needle and thread obviously represent a statement. But even more importantly, his unequivocal claim that his clothes are 'unwearable' has played a significant part in the creation of his reputation as a pariah, a 'provocateur', a maverick designer of a gimmicky style apparently irrelevant to the functions of dress in the second half of the twentieth century.

However, Paco Rabanne's investigative approach itself is far from irrelevant, and today, at the end of the millennium, is largely vindicated; it all began in the effervescent, forward-looking sixties, and even today the focus of his early work is strikingly appropriate: a re-evaluation of materials, respect for the environment, the accessibility of 'style', and an exploratory and radical approach to decorative effects in clothing.

t he sixties was a period of confrontation, in all spheres. Different terms of reference were introduced, deliberately at the opposite extreme to those established by previous generations. The baby-boom generation was looking for new values, independent of the past; youth became an advantage, the standard whose rules governed all behaviour.

Art turned its back on centuries-old procedures; painters abandoned canvas and brush, and sculptors gave up using stone and clay, in favour of other media and in pursuit of new, shared aesthetic goals, committed to a society focused on the future.

In this heady atmosphere, the existence of a new young clientele (no longer exclusively bourgeois), combined with the emergence of new couturiers of a similar age, had an impact on fashion that caused a radical change of direction.

The supremacy of haute couture and its right to dictate looks and rules was the most important thing to be called into question. At the fore-front were the new fashion leaders, known as 'stylists', whose influence eclipsed that of the great couturiers when they became the focus of media attention. In France, designers such as Daniel Hechter, Michèle Rosier, Emanuelle Khanh or Christiane Bailly offered their talents and fresh vision to clothing manufacturers, producing easy-to-wear fashion made in new materials and lively colours. At the same time, unconventional couturiers also established themselves: Courrèges, Saint Laurent, Cardin and Ungaro, amongst others, were becoming more important than their famous masters.

P aco Rabanne became part of this radically altered world as an independent designer; he was neither a stylist – although he played a part in the invention of the new 'style' with the extra-ordinary accessories he made for his friends – nor a couturier. However, in 1971, he was formally admitted to the Chambre Syndicale de la Couture.

It is hard to categorize Paco Rabanne because the course of his career and the nature of his work broke so completely with convention. A renegade architect, he was a compulsive designer, alternately producing handbags for Roger Model and shoes for the manufacturer Charles Jourdan; he made buttons and little accessories for haute couture houses, and at one time even made embroideries, before he became famous for his costume jewelry, and learned a great deal about material suppliers in the process.

He made a point of calling himself a craftsman, because of the importance he attached to manual skills. However, his influence on the history of fashion amounts to more than this emphasis on craftsmanship and the way things are made as this only partly explains the originality of his approach.

The key to what was to become a very definite style probably lies in his architectural training and his voracious appetite for contemporary technical innovations. Through architecture, Paco Rabanne learned to evaluate volume, understand space, and above all to follow the nature of the materials used, so that he was equipped to avoid the mistakes of a superficial approach.

It is now recognized that the most original aspect of his work, which drew equal amounts of praise and criticism at the time, was his determination to break new ground in exploring clothing design, and he has made a noticeable impact on the work of a young and successful second generation today.

'A force for deconstruction'

Although, provocative and an exaggeration, this is how the couturier described himself in 1969 – an accurate view of his role as he saw it. Even though the sixties are regarded as having challenged conformity in all areas, they are sometimes seen as having caused an impasse. With a solid grounding in haute couture learned from his mother, formerly chief seamstress with Balenciaga in Spain, Paco Rabanne was well placed to make a radical and cynical assessment of high fashion: 'What we create can only be a game, because fashion serves no purpose', he declared. 'But the society we live in always expects us to provide something new, so let us keep changing, constantly inventing "zany" things, as mad as possible! Fundamentally, I want to be a force for deconstruction.' (*Le Fait Public*, March 1969)

That was his aim and he sought to achieve it by a process of experimentation with the use of new materials, and particularly with innovative ways of using existing ones. From the early earrings made from Rhodoïd to the most recent dresses made with 'masks' from slide holders or using fibre optics, as well as the famous designs made with aluminium and the 'throwaway' paper dresses, Paco Rabanne has followed a consistent path, simultaneously examining the phenomenon of fashion and undermining assumptions about clothes.

Fashion as an ideological commitment

The 'zany' accessories, such as earrings, hairbands and belts, which catapulted Paco Rabanne onto the pages of the fashion magazines in 1965 were a huge media and commercial success, and originated with his interest in materials and the environment which he has maintained throughout his career.

The material used for these first designs was Rhodoïd, a rigid plastic, chosen very deliberately. It was light, cheap, and made in sheets of all colours; it could be cut into geometric units and perforated, then joined with metal rings to make playful earrings, light in spite of their large size, brightly coloured and inexpensive: they were made specifically for a young clientele, eager for something new. The material was capable of infinite combinations of form and colour, and could be used to mirror the effects produced by Op Art, which was regarded as the essence of modernity.

t he stunning success of these pieces (more than 25,000 were ordered in one year) heralded the arrival of a style of which Paco Rabanne was to be the standard bearer: it was based on the claim that cheap costume jewelry could have an aesthetic of its own, without hiding behind the imitation of something else. 'We are still making costume jewelry with paste, gilded metal and cut stones. Horrible! There is nothing worse than designers who make fake jewelry by aping the genuine. When a gem is fake, it should be obvious from twenty metres away.' (*Le Figaro littéraire*, 21 April 1966)

Encouraged by this early success, Paco Rabanne experimented with making 'little numbers', such as boleros, using the technique which was

9

to become the basis of all his designs, and using the same materials. Avant-garde shops such as Dorothée took them up immediately, and the fashion magazines, led by *Vogue*, prophesied the arrival of a new kind of garment which would 'replace the old "little black dress"' (*Vogue*, November 1965) – a pronouncement which immediately had the ring of authority.

A complete change in attitudes

On 1 February 1966 the twelve 'unwearable dresses in contemporary materials' were shown by barefoot models in a reception room at the Georges V Hotel, in Paris, to the accompaniment of Pierre Boulez's 'Marteau sans maître', and provoked divided reactions from the assembled journalists and professional buyers; both enthusiasm and consternation also greeted Paco Rabanne's subsequent shows and events, notably the 'happening' that was organized on the stage at the Crazy Horse Saloon in Paris. Barely three months after his first 'manifesto' collection, Paco Rabanne chose the resident artistes to present his designs. Wearing miners' helmets, Tracy Tiffany, Bettina Uranium, Prima Symphony and Bertha von Paraboum performed a classic strip-tease number, their outfits of discs and rectangles of Rhodoïd jangling.

'The designer of plastic fashion' was provocative, and was even sometimes regarded as a charlatan; nevertheless, he quickly became an undeniably important influence on fashion, and his work was widely publicized in the international press.

The deliberately irreverent tone of his statements, and the clarity of his observations on the fashion business and the way it operates attracted as much attention as his strange creations. 'Why should I want to compete with people who are already so good at cutting an outfit?' was his reply to those who criticized him for not making couture clothes. 'Who needs a new tailor? ... no one knows more about form than Balenciaga.'

Were his clothes unwearable? 'They are "manifesto" dresses', he replied, 'just as there are literary manifestos. By pushing certain experiences to the limit, it is possible to change people's attitudes.' (*Noir et Blanc*, 1967)

t he use of Rhodoïd and other rigid materials linked by metal rings or rivets destroyed the illusion created by a continuous fabric: the whole body could be seen through the gaps between the linked pieces, rather than just the limited areas exposed according to current ideas of feminine style. He also used lozenges of metal (an idea borrowed from butchers' aprons), rectangles of aluminium and even chain-mail, all intrinsically uncomfortable to wear: heavy, scalding in the heat, freezing in the cold. But when adapted for use in clothing, metal can shine, resonating with each movement, and make a powerful impact on the wearer and those around her. 'My clothes are weapons. When they are fastened they make a sound like the trigger of a revolver.' (*Marie Claire*, 1967)

The change of attitude that Paco Rabanne called for came not only from questioning the relationship of the body to its outer covering of clothes, but also the means of production and distribution of fashion.

Paco Rabanne's single-piece garment 'Giffo' was created by spraying liquid plastic into a specially designed mould, and resulted from this political examination of the popularization of 'style'. The process was perfected in 1968 after three years of trials, and made the industrial production of clothes possible almost instantly: instead of requiring some five hundred individual operations, now only two (spraying into the mould and later removing the garment from it) were necessary to make one raincoat per minute. However, this proved to be too radical a break with traditional manufacturing and buying habits; although it had entailed considerable investment, the process was not a commercial success, and the designs remained prototypes that a few lucky people managed to buy for a handful of francs.

With the same desire to make fashion more accessible, Paco Rabanne launched his series of paper dresses in 1967, which were more successful. This soft, lightweight material, made fire-resistant and reinforced with a nylon backing, was particularly appropriate for an era of increasing foreign travel, which necessitated the ability to 'travel light' anywhere in the world.

Paper was already being used, particularly in the United States, for functional clothes such as housewives' overalls, and was regarded as a cheap alternative to textiles. But Paco Rabanne refused to treat it as a substitute for textiles, and instead of sewing the different parts of the garment together he used adhesive tape of different colours, which became a decorative element of the design. His inspiration had been architects' 'binding-machines', used to protect the edges of drawings, and he adapted and mechanized them for Anik Robelin's factory where the dresses were produced in large numbers.

Paco Rabanne was a great admirer of Marcel Duchamp, and like him concentrated on unusual materials and all kinds of prefabricated objects to achieve the results he wanted, as well as finding different uses for the materials and techniques more traditionally used in haute couture.

He tackled new ways of treating fur, feathers, lace and embroidery. His first design using fur, in 1966, was a pair of sunglasses made of black astrakhan and silver Rhodoïd: a surrealist response to the need for protection simultaneously from the cold, sunlight and eye contact. A year later, the Simon Frères fashion house commissioned him to design a collection using their fine leathers and Paco Rabanne created an exciting juxtaposition of leather and metal, again using the well-known lozenges from butchers' protective aprons. Although initially shocked, clients rushed to buy this innovative look.

The full extent of the iconoclastic designer's inventiveness was displayed in 1968 when he began to use knitted fur – a patented process, as were most of the structures and systems invented by Paco Rabanne. It consisted of knitting together strips of fur, 'so that offcuts and pieces of fur too small to use in a traditional way can be made into a flexible, light and reversible material'. (*Bulletin Officiel de la Propriété Industrielle*, no. 13, 28 March 1969) The coats, capes, tunics and even trousers produced in this way had the added advantage of being both light and warm.

In 1966 feathers appeared on some of the outfits that were shown in Iris Clert's gallery in rue du Faubourg-Saint Honoré, Paris. The gallery owner, well known for her unconventional taste, chose to show these clothes in a context that emphasized the shared aesthetic concerns of the couturier in his experimental work and those of his artist contemporaries; for instance, a coat of white ostrich feathers attached with transparent bands of adhesive tape was displayed beside an oval painting by Lucio Fontana. In 1968 dresses and capes made of lattices of card or transparent plastic squares with dried flowers sealed inside them frequently had wisps of ostrich feather attached to them in this way, the soft fringes highlighting the sensuality of the partly concealed body.

ace was the next material to be re-evaluated, in spite of being one of the least likely to interest a designer committed to modern materials – it conjures up an image of femininity diametrically opposed to the aesthetic evolved by Paco Rabanne. Perhaps it was sheer perversity that influenced his choice at a time when lace was nowhere to be seen in most couturiers' collections. He perfected the process he used at the height of his fame in 1969: the lace was cut out, pressed between two layers of plastic, and linked with rings and circles of coloured Rhodoïd, or riveted to a dress made of metal pieces, so that sometimes the lace itself was almost unrecognizable.

Among the many old and valued skills used in the manufacture of luxury clothing, the application of embroidered decoration has traditionally been the most prized in haute couture, and has allowed the highest prices to be charged. Paradoxically, this was the very means Paco Rabanne chose in the early sixties to make an impact on the closed world of couture. With his eccentric treatment of applied decoration, he questioned not only the craft itself, but its high cost – a frequent goad to his creativity. Substituting rivets for sewing, beads and sequins were attached to the cloth with tiny studs and finished with a bow. In this way decoration could be added to a made-up garment relatively quickly.

The originality of the process and its low cost commanded respect among couturiers such as Maggy Rouff, Gérard Pipart at Nina Ricci, and Philippe Venet for the little atelier consisting of Paco Rabanne, his mother, and brothers and sisters, and the couturiers all commissioned him to make evening dresses. One of the decorated coats made of large lozenges of Rhodoïd for Philippe Venet was featured in the English and American editions of *Vogue* in July 1966, specifically crediting Paco Rabanne with the applied decoration.

'Creation does not mean seduction, it means impact'

Coco Chanel refused to count Paco Rabanne among the ranks of couturiers, labelling him a 'metal worker' – his work could be characterized by materials adapted from their original use, and techniques applied for a new purpose, but if her pointed witticism had some truth in it, it did not succeed in reducing his work to the status of one of the passing crazes that fashion is so fond of; on the contrary, it has stood the test of time and he has never deviated from his aims.

Paco Rabanne 'eccentricities' that connoisseurs of late twentieth-century fashion still enjoy include an aluminium jersey dress (1968), dresses made of buttons (1970), outfits made with handkerchiefs (1971), garments with sleeves made from socks (1973) and some composed of bands of woven rubber (1976), plastic waistcoats moulded to the body (1973), etc., but to try to define this unconventional couturier with an inventory of his accomplishments, however appreciative, would be to misunderstand his aims.

'What frightens me most about fashion is the occasions when too many people tell me they have liked my collection, because for me the originality lies in refusal, rejection. Creation does not mean seduction, it means impact. I aim to create moments of emotion, because emotion is truthful. It is the divine part of creation.'

This was how Paco Rabanne ended one of our last conversations, in March 1995. This solemnly whispered confidence illuminated, in particular, one of his youthful pronouncements that had puzzled me for a long time: 'My dresses made of metal clarify women's vision.'

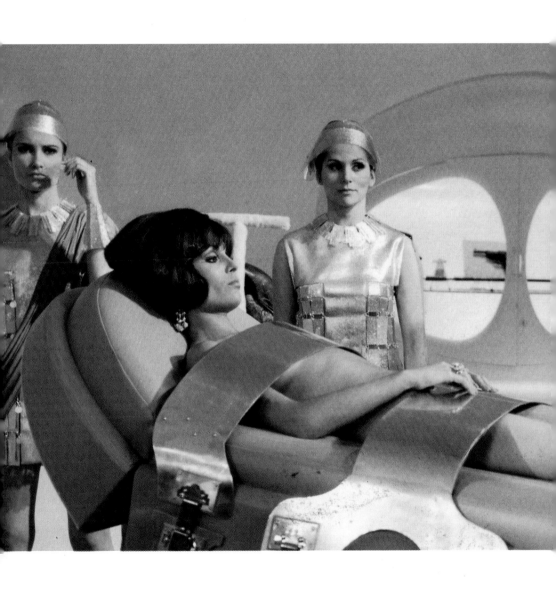

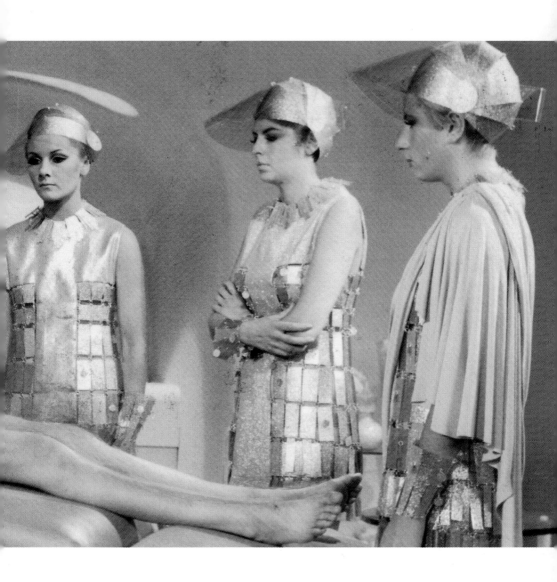

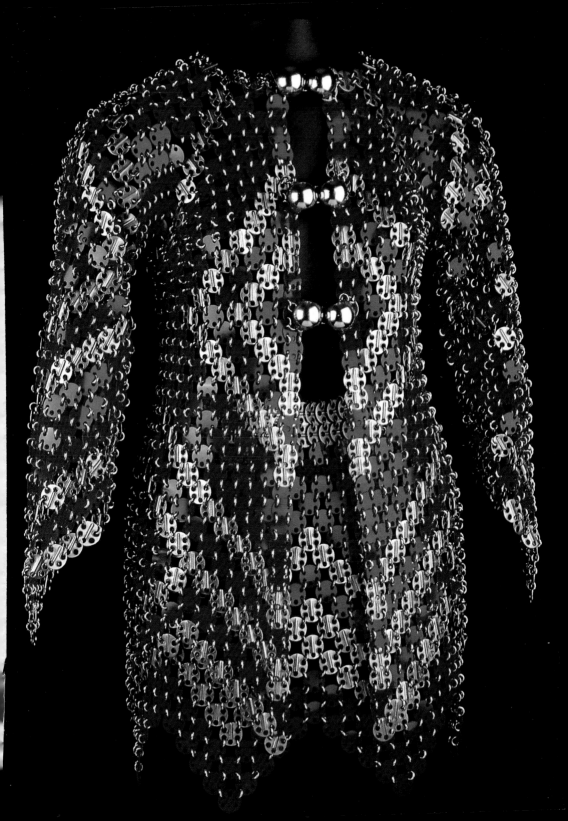

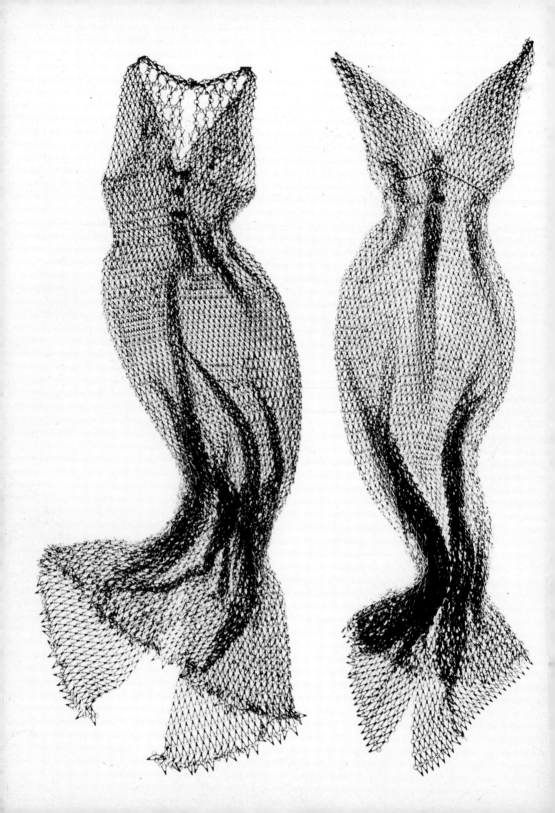

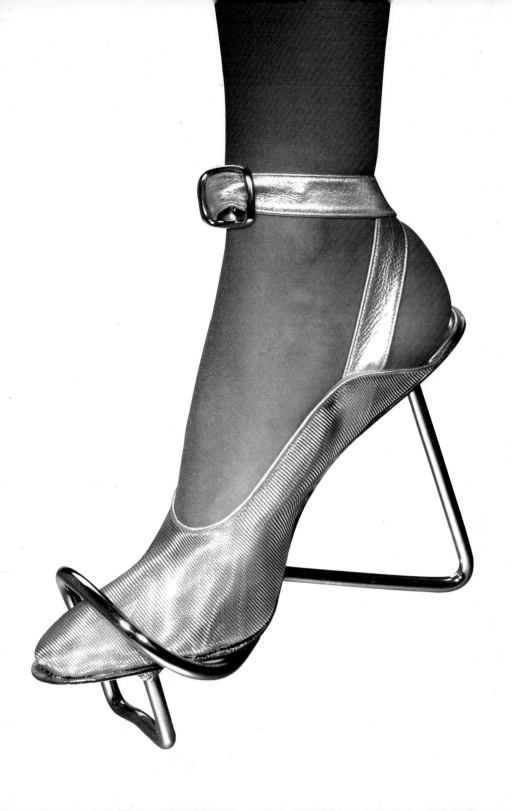

Chronology

1934	Birth of Francisco Rabaneda y Cuervo at Pasagès de San Pedro, in the Spanish Basque country.
1939	After the capture and execution of his father by pro-Franco troops, his family takes refuge in France. They settle in Morlaix and then Sables-d'Olonne.
1951–1963	Studies architecture at the Ecole Nationale Supérieure des Beaux-Arts in Paris.
1955–1963	Designs handbags for Roger Model and shoes for Charles Jourdan.
1959	*Women's Wear Daily* publishes seven sketches of his dress designs – strongly influenced by Balenciaga – signed 'Franck Rabanne'.
1962–1966	Makes buttons and embroidered decorations for haute couture houses (including Nina Ricci, Balenciaga, Maggy Rouff, Philippe Venet, Pierre Cardin and Givenchy).
1963	Wins prize at the Paris Biennale for his inhabitable garden sculpture, shown at the Musée d'Art Moderne in Paris.
1965	Makes accessories with Rhodoïd (earrings, glasses, helmets); works in collaboration with Michèle Rosier, Christiane Bailly and Emanuelle Khanh. First use of the name 'Paco Rabanne'.
1966	1 February, first 'manifesto' collection, with twelve 'unwearable dresses' made of discs and squares of Rhodoïd, shown at the Georges V Hotel in Paris. 21 April, a collection of beachwear in Rhodoïd is presented at the Crazy Horse Saloon, Paris, by resident artistes. In September, exhibition at Iris Clert's gallery, Paris, of designs using leather, ostrich feathers and aluminium. In October, Paco Rabanne opens his showroom at 33 rue Bergère, Paris. Produces costume designs for films: *Deux ou trois choses que je sais d'elle*, directed by Jean-Luc Godard, *Les Aventuriers*, directed by Robert Enrico, and *Two for the Road*, directed by Stanley Donen.
1967	Paper dresses; a fur collection for Simon Frères; first use of metal lozenges made for protective aprons; styles in fluorescent and riveted leather, and in aluminium. Makes dresses for the James Bond girls in the film *Casino Royale*, directed by John Huston.
1968	Beaten metal; aluminium jersey; knitted fur; dress made with gold and diamanté fabric for Arnaud Clerc; 'Giffo' mould-made garment. Licence to produce Rabanne perfumes awarded to the Spanish group Puig.
1969	Lozenges like the ones used for protective aprons produced in Rhodoïd. Creation of ten 'Rob-auto' ready-to-wear designs for Heko. Launch of the perfume Calandre. Pierre Belfond publishes *Nues*, an interview with Paco Rabanne, with photographs by Jean Clemmer.
1970	Dresses made of linked buttons.
1971	Designs made of Cholet handkerchiefs; notched seams and inlaid rivets. Admission to the Chambre Syndicale de la Couture. Opens his couture house at 7 rue du Cherche-Midi, Paris.
1972	Designs with interchangeable decorations made of ostrich feathers and attached with velcro. Launch of 'Paco' shoes.
1973	Pattens and bags in rigid moulded plastic; sleeves of jumpers made from socks; masks and bustiers in transparent moulded plastic. Launch of the perfume Paco Rabanne pour Homme.
1976	First ready-to-wear collection for men. Launch of retail collection intended to be a classic formula: basic designs continue from one season to the next with changes in materials and colours. Opening of the Paco Rabanne perfume factory at Chartres, France.

The singer Françoise Hardy wearing a swimsuit of white Rhodoïd. © J.-M. Périer/Elle.

1977   Variations on a shawl/dress theme.

Awarded the Aiguille d'Or.

Contract with Sogo to make clothes by Paco Rabanne under licence in Japan.

1978   African 'boubous' printed with the image of Giscard d'Estaing, following the French President's visit to Africa; dresses made of round and oval wooden beads.

1979   Opening of a franchised shop for men's wear at 30 boulevard des Italiens, Paris.

Launch of the perfume Métal.

1981   Launch of La Maison de Paco Rabanne – a franchised chain of furniture and interior design shops – in collaboration with Julien Ayache.

1982   Dresses made with glass reflectors.

1983   Creation of Centre 57 – a private initiative by Paco Rabanne – which provided support and work space for black artists, based in a disused hot air balloon factory at 57 boulevard de la Villette, Paris.

1984   Chain-mail doublets and long pointed shoes 'à la poulaine'.

Launch of a range of toiletries for men.

1985   Design of 'KIT' line, using stiff top-stitched interfacing, assembled with press studs.

Launch of the perfume La Nuit.

1986   Fitted fur coats, boleros with flowers made of fox and mink, made by Révillon; four dresses made with painted discs, inspired by Georges de la Tour's painting *Le Tricheur à l'As de Carreau (Cheat with the Ace of Diamonds)*.

The couture house is bought by the Puig group.

Launch of Sport, a perfume for men.

1988   Dresses in metallic iridescent paper, and designs made using linked pieces of laser discs.

The film *Salaam Bombay*, directed by Mira Nair and produced by Paco Rabanne, is awarded the Camera d'Or at the Cannes Film Festival.

1989   Vertical 'ballerina' shoes with integral 20 cm high heels.

Launch of the men's perfume Ténéré.

1990   Use of lamé made with laser-treated reflecting fabric.

Awarded the Dé d'Or for his spring/summer collection.

Launch of a women's ready-to-wear range.

Opening of the boutique at 7 rue du Cherche-Midi, Paris.

1991   'Lofo' dresses of iridescent paper backed with tulle and decorated with large fake jewels; dresses of linked mirror discs and of material coated with liquid crystals.

1992   Dresses of iridescent pleated rubber; a 'Spanish' range – toreadors' boleros and Sevillian dresses – to commemorate the World Fair at Seville, Spain; tube dresses of woven transparent rubber.

1993   Dresses made using fibre optics; launch of the perfume XS.

Michel Lafon publishes *La Fin des temps*.

1994   Plexiglas dresses; shoes without heels.

Launch of the perfume XS pour Elle.

Launch, with *Elle* magazine, of a small case containing a dress in kit form.

Michel Lafon publishes *Temps présent*.

1995   Garments made from bands of elastic, a backward glance at his 1976 collection.

Launch of a collection with the *3 Suisses*.

In June to September, first exhibition of the work of Paco Rabanne at the Musée de la Mode in Marseille, France.

1996   Launch of the Paco concept: a unisex perfume in a recyclable aluminium container and a range of 'timeless' clothes.

Michel Lafon publishes *Paco Rabanne: les sens de la recherche*, by Lydia Kamitsis, in a French/English bi-lingual edition.

A sheath of chain mail, paste and multi-coloured metal, photographed by David Seidner, and published in Elle *magazine, 3 February 1997. © David Seidner.*

Paco Rabanne

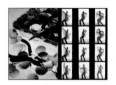

A self-assembly Paco Rabanne design kit in a transparent case; the kit consists of 750 discs, 1,300 rings, a metal label and two pairs of pliers. © Sicot.
'Photographing an almost naked woman is true eroticism: it is not nudity itself that is erotic, but the covering which veils it and allows it to be partly revealed. Display draws attention to the body and provokes, whereas a garment hides it', Paco Rabanne discussing the book *Nues* (1969). © Jean Clemmer.

Paco Rabanne's Rhodoïd earrings, launched in 1965, lifted him out of obscurity. The variety of designs made possible by an infinite combination of colours and shapes captivated a clientele and fashion press avid for novelty. Nearly 25,000 were sold around the world. © Paco Rabanne Archives.

The availability of Rhodoïd in a wide range of colours stimulated Paco Rabanne's imagination. This dress made of discs is decorated with pearlized, iridescent 'petals' adding to the 'dressy' effect (1967). © Paco Rabanne Archives.

Outsize earrings in *Vogue*, 1966. © Condé Nast Publications Ltd.
Two-coloured tunic (ready-to-wear, spring/summer 1997). © Christophe Kutner.

The past master of provocation, Salvador Dalí, was captivated by his young fellow countryman's work and called him 'Spain's second genius'; here, he poses surrounded by models wearing Paco Rabanne's 'unwearable dresses in contemporary materials'. The glasses with individually hinged lenses, made in 1965, are a surrealist version of a 'wink'. © Paco Rabanne Archives.

A grid made of rigid elements linked with metal rings is both a contradiction of the idea of a continuous length of cloth, and the means of making a clothing fabric out of any material that can be perforated. © Michel Béchet.
Paco Rabanne's trademark became, to some extent, this way of making a garment; here, Audrey Hepburn is wearing one of his dresses in the 1966 film *Two for the Road*, directed by Stanley Donen. © Collection Christophe L.

Photographers' personal interpretations of Paco Rabanne's 'photogenic' designs.
Dress as a hat by photographer Georges Tourdjman (1966). © Georges Tourdjman.
Bolero (autumn/winter collection 1995–1996). © Photo Philippe Chevalier.

'He's not a couturier, but a metal worker': Paco Rabanne makes fun of Coco Chanel's terse epithet. © Keystone.

Twiggy wearing a motorcycling-style outfit made of metal riveted onto leather (1967). © Traeger/*Elle*.

The triangle: two ways of using the same geometrical motif and the same means of construction to achieve different results.

Coat lined with borg fake fur (winter 1966–1967). © Paco Rabanne Archives.

Fluorescent leather dress developed by Patrick Lavoix for the Puy tanneries in 1967. © Paco Rabanne Archives.

'Rodéo', a leather dress forming part of the collection shown on shop window dummies at Iris Clert's gallery, Paris, in September 1966. © Keystone.

This dress of linked pieces of leather is still perfectly 'cut', as can be seen in the shape of the neck and the square pieces forming the armholes. Photo Gunnar Larsen. © Galerie Weitz.

The futuristic sets of some sixties films are based on Paco Rabanne's style. Shown here are the dresses and helmets made of linked pieces designed for *Casino Royale*, a James Bond film directed in 1967 by John Huston. © Photo Paris Presse.

The mannequin Verushka posing as a modern Amazon in a dress with strategically placed cut-outs (autumn/winter 1968–1969). © Franco Rubartelli/ *Vogue*.

The most photographed of Paco Rabanne's designs, and the best illustration of the impact he made on followers of fashion. Mini dress of aluminium squares with added flowers and buttons of the same material (1968). Photo Gunnar Larsen. © Galerie Weitz.

Butcher's protective aprons, made of metal circles or squares overlapping like scales, were the basis of Paco Rabanne's first major reinterpretation. © Michel Béchet.

The theme is carried through to the décor of his first showroom, 33 rue Bergère, Paris, composed of steel scaffolding with furniture consisting of bicycle saddles and cinema seats. © Photographic Service.

From reinterpretation to transposition: two features of Paco Rabanne's work.
In 1968 he added a lavatory chain to a handbag, a reference to Marcel Duchamp's 'ready-mades', and an irreverent homage to Coco Chanel's famous chain handbag strap. © Paco Rabanne Archives.
In 1969 the metal lozenges originally made for butcher's aprons were adapted and made in other materials such as coloured Rhodoïd. © Stéphane Cicerone.

Long coat with crocheted edges, posed in front of a building by Ricardo Bofill (1979). Aluminium jersey (like 'squam', which Paco Rabanne was the first to use for making clothes) shows the virtuosity of the couturier who could turn this demanding material into majestically hanging, supple dresses. © Jean Loup Sieff.
Mini dress (autumn/winter 1967–1968). © Paco Rabanne Archives.

Shawl-effect bolero of steel chain-mail, with black fringe; design from the autumn/winter collection 1978–1979, used in publicity material for the opening of the Paco Rabanne boutique at 7 rue du Cherche-Midi, Paris, in 1990. Photo Patrick Ibanez. © All Rights Reserved.

Headdress with beaded fringe veil (autumn/winter 1990–1991). Photo Peter de Mulder. © All Rights Reserved.
Wedding dress in rectangles of opalescent Rhodoïd (1966). © Georges Tourdjman.

Over three decades, Paco Rabanne's clothes have softened and lightened, with a new sensual form which clings to the curves of the body.
Net-like mermaid dress in metallized plastic (1994). Photo Mark Malttock. © All Rights Reserved.
'Body' in discs of transparent Rhodoïd highlighted with paste details (spring/summer 1991). © Bruno Bisang.

Evening dress with a bodice of chromium-plated steel chain-mail and wide bouffant skirt of gold lamé (1986). © Keiichi Tahara.

'Giffo' mould-made garment, using the revolutionary method developed in 1968. © Jean Clemmer.
Sewn vinyl dress with gold-chain shoulder straps (ready-to-wear, spring/summer 1995). © Manzetti.

78

In the hands of Paco Rabanne, fur is freed from its traditional overtones of bourgeois luxury.
Fox tails made into appliqué flowers (1966). © Paco Rabanne Archives.
Cape in knitted Dralon (1968). © Guy Bourdin.

Paper, as a disposable material, has its own formal possibilities which Paco Rabanne has explored since 1967, when he made his first 'throwaway' dress. © All Rights Reserved.
Design in metallized pleated paper (summer 1992). © Gilles Bensimon.

The art of volume is clearly shown in these winter coats of 1989–1990: they combine architectural qualities with the discipline of Balenciaga, which Paco Rabanne has admired from his very early years. © Michel Béchet.

From the early aluminium dresses to the most recent ones in fibre optics, by way of the many reflectors, holograms and laser discs in between, Paco Rabanne's career often seems like a preoccupation with light.
Dress decorated with fibre optics (summer 1993). © Guy Marineau.
'Fountain' dress made of plastic tubes (winter 1993–1994). © Paco Rabanne Archives.

Contrasting empty and filled space.
Dresses in iridescent plastic (summer 1992). © Stéphane Cicerone.
Court shoe in metal netting on a metal base (spring/summer 1996). © Michel Béchet.

Bikini made from metal jewelry parts for Naomi Campbell, transformed into an android mutant (top: summer 1989; thong: summer 1991; shoes: summer 1996). © Seb Janiak.

In 1996 the perfume Paco was launched, bridging the gap between the sexes: the container is made of recyclable aluminium, in keeping both with the couturier's work and his ecological concerns. © Paco Rabanne Archives.
Calandre was the key perfume of an earlier period: for its launch in 1969 its new concept of style was linked with this archetypal dress made of alternate smooth and beaten metal pieces. © Stéphane Cicerone.

The publishers would like to thank members of the Paco Rabanne company, particularly Mariano Puig, Gilbert Personeni and Rolande Pozo, and the press department for their help in the production of this book.

Thanks also to Françoise Hardy, Verushka, Twiggy Lawssen, Naomi Campbell, Jean Loup Sieff, Georges Tourdjman, Gilles Bensimon, Patrick Ibanez, Bruno Bisang, Jean Clemmer, Michel Béchet, Christophe Kutner, Seb Janiak, Stéphane Cicerone, Patrice Stable and Chrystèle Saint-Louis Augustin.

Lastly, the publication of this book would not have been possible without the generous co-operation of the Weitz Gallery, Samuel Bourdin, Ruth Eagleton (of Condé Nast Publications Ltd), Sandrine Bizarro (of Filomeno), Marc Plussenier, Laurent Rojot, Claudine Legros (of *Elle*/Scoop), Albert (of Keystone) and Josianne Ségo (of *France Soir*).

Many thanks to all of them.